# Police
**Then and Now**

**Melissa A. Settle, M.Ed.**

**Associate Editor**
Christina Hill, M.A.

**Assistant Editor**
Torrey Maloof

**Editorial Director**
Emily R. Smith, M.A.Ed.

**Project Researcher**
Gillian Eve Makepeace

**Editor-in-Chief**
Sharon Coan, M.S.Ed.

**Editorial Manager**
Gisela Lee, M.A.

**Creative Director**
Lee Aucoin

**Illustration Manager**
Timothy J. Bradley

**Designers**
Lesley Palmer
Debora Brown
Zac Calbert
Robin Erickson

**Project Consultant**
Corinne Burton, M.A.Ed.

**Publisher**
Rachelle Cracchiolo, M.S.Ed.

*Teacher Created Materials*

5301 Oceanus Drive
Huntington Beach, CA 92649-1030
http://www.tcmpub.com
**ISBN 978-0-7439-9372-2**
© 2007 Teacher Created Materials, Inc.

# Table of Contents

# Who Are the Police?

Police officers (AH-fuh-suhrz) work as a team. When one job is done, they have to go to the next one. They work hard all day and all night long.

Police officers are people who are trained to "protect and serve." That means they help keep people safe. It also means they help make sure that people obey **laws**. Police officers work in small towns and big cities. They drive cars, walk, and even ride bicycles and horses.

⬇ Police officers drive special cars.

A police officer ➡ on his horse in the 1920s.

♦ Police officers used to ride bicycles.

♦ Some officers still ride bicycles today.

◆ Police officers stop a driver for speeding.

# Patrolling the Streets

Some police officers have to **patrol** (puh-TROLL) the streets. This means they watch for crimes. They go to the **scenes** of any crimes. There, they help the **victims** (vik-TUHMZ).

There are many types of patrol officers. Some are traffic officers. They make sure that drivers follow the rules. These officers drive patrol cars or ride on motorcycles. In small towns, the sheriff's deputies keep the streets safe. State troopers **enforce** the laws on large freeways or highways.

These officers help people in other ways, too. They help children who are lost. They direct traffic if there is an accident. They even stop fights between people. These brave men and women help in any way they can to make the streets safe.

▲ Texas Rangers, 1842

## Dangerous Jobs

Every police job is dangerous. But, there are some that are very dangerous. Members of the bomb squad risk their lives every day. Their job is to find and get rid of bombs safely. They have to be very careful. And, they must be brave.

## Early Police Officers

About 200 years ago, a group of men worked to keep the people of Texas safe. They were known as the Texas Rangers. There are many stories, books, and movies about the brave Texas Rangers.

# Police Around the World

The world's first police **department** was started in London, England. Sir Robert Peel started it in 1829. To honor him, British police officers are called "bobbies."

Ireland has some police officers who do not carry weapons. When they patrol the streets, they do not have guns. They trust that people will do what they say.

▲ This police officer works in a train station in Japan.

In India, police officers drive jeeps and motorcycles. These make it easier for them to get around.

In Japan, police get along with the people. The people trust the police. Police officers are often asked for help. The police give directions. They even give advice to children.

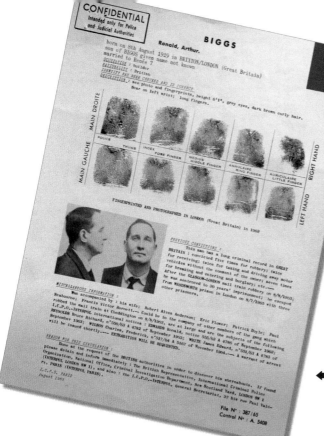

BIGGS

Ronald, Arthur.

born on 8th August 1929 in BRIXTON/LONDON (Great Britain)
son of BIGGS given name not known
married to Renée ?

## Interpol

There is a group that helps find criminals all over the world. It is called the International Criminal Police Organization. It is known as Interpol (in-TUHR-puhl). This group works with many countries.

◄Interpol uses this information to catch a criminal.

▼ A police car in England

## Jam Sandwich?

Some people in England call the police cars "jam sandwiches." The cars are white. But, across the middle of each car is a big orange stripe. So, it looks like a sandwich!

# Police Detectives and Crime Labs

Police **detectives** (dih-TEK-tivs) work hard to solve crimes. This is how they catch **criminals** (KRIM-uh-nuhlz). Most criminals make mistakes. The detectives look for **clues**. Then, they piece together the clues like a puzzle. When they have all the pieces, they catch the criminals.

↟ A police officer dusts for fingerprints.

↡ A man being fingerprinted in the 1930s

## Fingerprints

Every person has a set of prints on their fingers. Those prints are **unique** (you-NEEK). Unique means that no two are the same. The prints on your fingers will be the same your whole life. They never change.

Some criminals leave **evidence** (EHV-uh-duhntz) when they break the law. It might be hair, blood, or **fingerprints**. Detectives have special tools to find these things.

These officers send what they find to a crime lab. Then, the crime lab workers start working! They use computers and special machines to help them. It takes a long time to do the work.

The crime lab workers tell the detectives what they find. Then, the detectives use all the clues to catch the criminals.

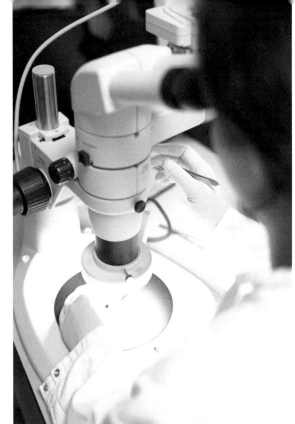

⬆ Microscopes (MY-kruh-skopes) are used to see small samples of evidence.

## Television Crime Fighters

Have you seen any television shows about the police? People like to see how police detectives solve crimes. They like to try and put together all the clues. Everyone likes a good mystery!

↓ D.A.R.E. program

# Police Officers Working with Kids

There is a special program called D.A.R.E. It stands for Drug Abuse **Resistance** (rih-ZIS-tuhntz) Education. Special D.A.R.E. officers visit classrooms. They teach students how to say no to drugs. Usually, D.A.R.E. starts in fifth or sixth grade. Do you have D.A.R.E. at your school?

It's fun to → turn on a police car's lights and sirens.

## Visits from the Law!

Some police officers visit schools. They like to show the students their patrol cars and tools. Students can even sit in the cars and run the sirens.

♠ This police helicopter visits a school.

There are other officers who help kids. **Juvenile** (JUH-vuh-nyl) officers are special police officers. They work only with young people. Many children have problems at home or in school. These officers help solve those problems. They work hard to protect children.

# Who Helps the Police?

Do you know what 9-1-1 is for? It is a special phone number. It is used only in an **emergency**. Operators will answer these calls. They need to know where, when, and what has happened.

Then, the 9-1-1 operator will call a police **dispatcher** (dis-PACH-uhr). The dispatcher sends a police officer to help the people in need.

School crossing guards also help the police. They help kids to safely cross the streets. This helps to control traffic. That way, there are fewer accidents.

This operator answers ➤ a 9-1-1 call.

▲ The Secret Service guards
President Theodore Roosevelt.

## Secret Service Then and Now

The first Secret Service group began in 1865. The Secret Service made sure that people did not make fake money. Today, the Secret Service has a different job. They work to protect the president and other leaders.

## Lots of Letters

FBI stands for Federal Bureau of Investigation. FBI agents fight crime just like police officers do. They work all across the country. CIA stands for Central Intelligence Agency. They try to stop crimes, too. They work all around the world.

# Female Officers

Women used to only work inside the police station. They answered phones and filled out forms. They were not allowed to patrol the street. People thought the streets were too dangerous. They did not want women to get hurt.

The women were called police matrons. They could not arrest people. Alice S. Wells changed this in 1910. She worked in Los Angeles, California. Ms. Wells became the first female police officer who could arrest people.

Now, people realize that women can be good officers. They are strong and brave. They work hard to keep people safe.

Today, many police ➡ officers are women.

# Women in London

The first female police officers were hired in London in 1949. But, they were not allowed to work the night shift. Today, female police officers can work any shift.

▲ A policewoman in London

# A Female Detective

Mary Shanley earned the nickname "Dead Shot Mary." She was a patrol officer in New York. She made over 1,000 arrests! Ms. Shanley proved that women could be good police officers. In 1935, she became a police detective.

Detective Mary Shanley is ➡ congratulated by the mayor.

# Technology Changes Things

Most police officers used to walk or ride horses. They took people to jail in wagons. After that, the police started to use bicycles. Then, they began to use cars and motorcycles.

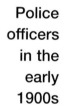

Police officers in the early 1900s →

◀ Motorcycles help police officers move easily through traffic.

Police officers did not always use radios. The officers had to stay at the police station. They would wait for calls to come in. Then, the officers would drive to the crime. It took a long time. So, many criminals got away. This was a problem!

All kinds of ideas were tried. One idea was to have police officers wait in phone booths for calls. This did not work well. Then, someone thought to use radios. At first, police radios only let people listen. Now, officers can talk back and forth with radios.

## Patrol Car Computers

Did you know that patrol officers have computers in their cars? They use their computers when they pull people over. They enter your license plate number. Then, they can find out who you are.

## Four Hours?

The first police car radios had batteries. They had to be changed every four hours. That did not give them much time!

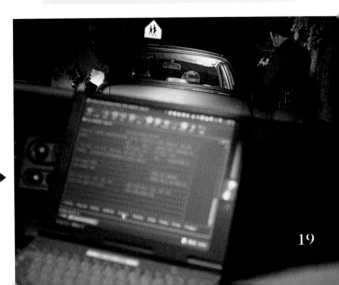

A computer inside ➡
a patrol car

# Animal Partners

There is a **canine** (KAY-nine) **unit** in many police stations. This means that police officers have dogs for partners. The dogs have to go to training schools. There, they learn how to obey the officers. Then, they can become police dogs.

The dogs also learn how to fight crime. They are trained to sniff for certain smells. They sniff to find

◄ This dog helps his partners protect others.

## Sign Language

A police dog has to learn to obey hand signals. Sometimes it might be too loud for the dog to hear his partner. He can also watch for signals if the team is trying to be quiet.

lost people. And, they even sniff to find drugs and weapons.

Some police officers ride horses. This way, they can see people in a big crowd. Horses also help the police look for people who are lost. But, the horses do not sniff for clues like the police dogs. The horses help the officers cover more area in a search.

◀ Horses are used to search for lost people.

## Are Cars Cleaner Than Horses?

Long ago in New York City, police officers rode horses. But, some people thought that cars would be cleaner. They were worried about the horse manure (muh-NYUR) in the city. Today, people worry about **pollution** (puhl-LUH-shuhn) from all the cars!

# Safe Communities

Not all police officers do the same job. Some officers drive cars. Others may ride horses or walk. Some officers have dogs as partners. Patrol officers work on city streets. But, deputy sheriffs work in small towns. And, detectives work to solve crimes.

◆ If this boy ever gets lost, the police will use his fingerprints to find him.

Each type of police officer is different. But, they all have something in common. Their jobs are important to us. They work to help our communities. By working together, they try to stop crime. This keeps our neighborhoods safe.

▼ This police officer directs traffic during a parade.

# A Day in the Life Then

**Wyatt Earp (1848–1929)**

The Old West was a dangerous time. There were few laws. There were no police departments. But, there were **lawmen**. They were like police officers. These men helped fight crime. Wyatt Earp (WHY-uht UHRP) and his brothers were lawmen. They helped keep people safe.

**Let's pretend to ask Wyatt Earp some questions about his job.**

**When did you decide to be a lawman?**

I did not always make good choices. I got in trouble with the law a few times. I learned my lesson. Now I know that it is important to have laws. I decided that I wanted to help the people in our town. So, I became a lawman.

## What is your job like?

I try to keep the town safe from outlaws. Outlaws are men who do not follow the laws. Every morning, I wake up and put on my badge. That way, people know I am there to keep them safe. I ride my horse through town. I make sure that the outlaws are not causing any trouble.

Legend has it that Mr. Earp saved this coach from being robbed.

## What do you like most about your job?

I like that I am helping to build a safe community. I live in a small town. People travel here to mine for gold. When people first came here, there were no laws. It was a very dangerous place to live. I hope that I can help to make our town a safer place for people to live.

# Tools of the Trade Then

▼ This is a jail cell from long ago. People were put in jail if they broke the law. This helped keep towns safe.

▲ This is one of the first female police officers. She wore a police uniform and a badge. The badge let others know that she was an officer. That way, people knew they could go to her for help.

Dogs helped ➤ police officers long ago. They helped solve crimes. Police dogs even saved people's lives!

# Tools of the Trade Now

Today, police officers have radios ➤ and other tools that help them speak to each other. They even have computers. And, their police cars help them travel very fast.

◀ Dogs are still important to police officers. This dog helps his partner solve crimes. They make a great team!

Today, detectives use ➤ fingerprints to solve crimes. This helps them catch criminals.

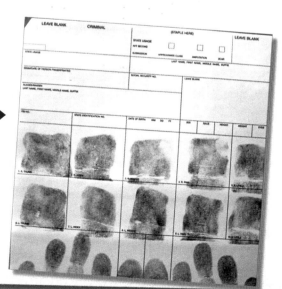

# A Day in the Life Now

**Steve Austin**

Steve Austin is a police officer in Broomfield, Colorado. He has been a police officer for 18 years. He works hard to keep his city safe. In his free time, Mr. Austin loves to go camping and hiking. He

enjoys spending time with his wife Sue and their two dogs, Okie-Dokie and Mr. Levi.

## Why did you decide to become a police officer?

I used to watch police shows on television when I was a kid. Being a police officer looked exciting. Then, when I grew up, I joined the United States

Air Force. I learned a lot. With my Air Force training, I thought I could be a good police officer.

## What is your day like?

My job is different every day. Sometimes, I patrol the city in my police car. I do this during the day. I follow up on any crimes that may have happened the night before. Sometimes people break the law. So, I work hard to try to stop these people. At night, I make sure that everybody in our city is safe.

## What do you like most about your job?

I like to help people. I also like when I get to speak to students at schools. I teach kids how to stay safe.

This is the inside ➡ of Mr. Austin's police car.

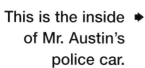

# Glossary

**canine unit**—a group of police dogs

**clues**—pieces of evidence

**criminals**—people who break the law

**department**—a group of people working for a common cause

**detectives**—people who try to solve crimes

**dispatcher**—person who answers emergency calls

**emergency**—a dangerous situation

**enforce**—to make sure things are done

**evidence**—materials left behind by a criminal that are used to solve a crime

**fingerprints**—marks made by ridges on a person's fingers

**juvenile**—a young person

**lawmen**—officers that enforce the law

**laws**—rules that people must follow

**patrol**—watching and guarding an area

**pollution**—chemicals and waste that harm the air and water

**resistance**—not giving in to something

**scenes**—the places of action

**unique**—different than others

**victims**—people who are hurt by others

# Index

# Credits

## Acknowledgements

Special thanks to Steve Austin for providing the *Day in the Life Now* interview. Mr. Austin is a police officer. He works at the Broomfield Police Department in the city and county of Broomfield, Colorado, headed by Chief Tom Deland.

## Image Credits

cover Corbis; p.1 Corbis; p.4 (left) Hemera Technologies, Inc; p.4 (right) Photos.com; p.5 (top) Denver Public Library, Western History Collection; p.5 (left) Photos.com; p.5 (right) iStockphoto.com/Tony Tremblay; p.6 Photos.com; p.7 (top) The Granger Collection, New York; p.7 (bottom) Hemera Technologies, Inc; p.8 Junji Kurokawa/AFP/Getty Images; p.9 (top) Getty Images; p.9 (bottom) Gareth Cattermole/Getty Images; p.10 (top) Hemera Technologies, Inc; p.10 (left) The Library of Congress; p.10 (right) Photos.com; p.11 BigStockPhoto; p.12 Superstock.com; p.13 (top) Photos.com; p.13 (bottom) iStockphoto.com/Terry Healy; p.14 (top) Photos.com; pp. 14–15 Rob Nelson/Time Life Pictures/Getty Images; p.15 The Library of Congress; p.16 Photos.com; p.17 (top) The Library of Congress; p.17 (bottom) The Library of Congress; p.18 (top) The Library of Congress; p.18 (bottom) iStockphotos.com/Matt Matthews; p.19 Photos.com; p.20 Photos.com; p.21 iStockphotos.com/Jocelyn Lin; p.22 David McNew/Getty Images; p.23 Cristiaciobanu/Dreamstime; p.24 The Granger Collection, New York; p.25 The Library of Congress; p.26 (top right) The Library of Congress; p.26 (top left) The Library of Congress; p.26 (bottom) The Library of Congress; p.27 (top) iStockphoto.com/Frances Twitty; p.27 (middle) BigStockPhoto; p.27 (bottom) Kevin L Chesson/Shutterstock, Inc.; p.28 Courtesy of Steve Austin; p.29 Courtesy of Steve Austin; back cover The Library of Congress